Author:
Fiona Macdonald studied history at
Cambridge University, England, and at the
University of East Anglia. She has taught in
schools, universities, and in adult education, and
is the author of numerous books for children on
historical topics.

Artist:
David Antram was born in Brighton, England,
in 1958. He studied at Eastbourne College of Art
and then worked in advertising for fifteen years
before becoming a full-time artist. He has
illustrated many children's nonfiction books.

Series creator:
David Salariya was born in Dundee, Scotland.
He has illustrated a wide range of books and has
created and designed many new series for
publishers in the UK and overseas. David
established The Salariya Book Company in 1989.
He lives in Brighton, England, with his wife,
illustrator Shirley Willis, and their son Jonathan.

Editor: Tanya Kant

Editorial Assistant: Mark Williams

Published in Great Britain in 2009 by
The Salariya Book Company Ltd
25 Marlborough Place, Brighton BN1 1UB

ISBN-13: 978-0-531-20822-9 (lib. bdg.)   978-0-531-21046-8 (pbk.)
ISBN-10: 0-531-20822-2 (lib. bdg.)   0-531-21046-4 (pbk.)

All rights reserved.
Published in 2009 in the United States
by Franklin Watts
An imprint of Scholastic Inc.
Published simultaneously in Canada.

A CIP catalog record for this book is available
from the Library of Congress.

Printed and bound in China.
Printed on paper from sustainable sources.

You Wouldn't Want to Meet a Body Snatcher!

This body is mingin!
(This body smells awful!)

Written by
Fiona Macdonald

Illustrated by
David Antram

Created and designed by
David Salariya

Criminals and Murderers You'd Rather Avoid

Franklin Watts®
An Imprint of Scholastic Inc.
NEW YORK • TORONTO • LONDON • AUCKLAND • SYDNEY
MEXICO CITY • NEW DELHI • HONG KONG
DANBURY, CONNECTICUT

Contents

Introduction
Edinburgh, Scotland, 1828

Welcome, stranger! Come on in! Join us! You'll find that this inn is nowhere special. It's just another tall, crooked house, with shabby rooms and dark, secret stairs. They're everywhere in Edinburgh's Old Town, huddled around shadowy closes (narrow streets or entries) or lining rat-infested wynds (alleys). But there's nowhere cozier on a bitter winter's night.

Who are we? Just a crowd of Edinburgh writers. We like to meet and discuss the news. As a journalist, I can tell you all the latest gossip—especially when it comes to body-snatching!

We're always excited to meet clever young men like yourself—students in our fine city. From the look of you, I'd say you are in training to become a doctor, or maybe a scientist. Have you made any exciting discoveries lately?

Come on in and tell us about yourself. Speak up— we're all listening!

Welcome, sir! Let me tell you all the latest Edinburgh news…

Well, young man, I was right, wasn't I? You're a medical student here in Edinburgh. You say that you've always been fascinated by anatomy, the study of bodies? Now, you want to be a doctor? You've come to the right city—Edinburgh is the very best place to study medicine!

Everyone knows that Edinburgh is the most exciting city in Europe, and its university is world-famous. Students travel here from distant lands—England, Ireland, Germany, even the United States. So many have arrived that a whole new lecture room, the Anatomy Theatre, has been built for them at the university, with seats for over 200 people!

Just one wee drop...

Old slums

OLD. Edinburgh's Old Town is Scotland's ancient capital. It has streets lined with tall, shabby houses. But there's also the magnificent Edinburgh Castle, a royal palace, and a Botanic Garden full of medicinal plants. The Old Town is full of history!

Surgeon's Square

Handy Hint

If you want to learn, join a club! How about Edinburgh's famous Poker Club? Its members "stir up" new ideas, just as a poker stirs up a fire.

NEW. Edinburgh's New Town is the modern quarter of the city, built during the past 50 years. The university and teaching hospital are here, as well as libraries, museums, and Surgeon's Square.

David Hume, philosopher

Robert Adam, architect

Robert Burns, poet

Adam Smith, philosopher

James Watt, inventor

GREAT MINDS. There's a famous saying about Edinburgh: "If you stand in the main street for an afternoon, you'll be able to shake 50 men of genius by the hand."

That sounds very boastful, but it's not far from the truth. Writers, thinkers, doctors, scientists, engineers—they've all taught or studied here! Their achievements are famous worldwide.

The Good Doctor

Observe the subject's heart, a vital organ that pumps blood around the body...

Young man, I must ask you: have you met Dr. Knox? He's one of Britain's most famous scientists. Popular and fashionable, he lives here in Edinburgh. They say he's a brilliant teacher who makes medicine fun. He has more than 500 students. To teach them all, he repeats each lecture three times!

Have you been to any of his demonstrations, where he dissects (cuts up) dead bodies and explains how the body works? What's that? You want to investigate bodies, just like Knox—and save lots of lives?

A Brilliant Career

AT SCHOOL, he wins a medal for being the best student.

THE YEAR after he gets his medical degree, he receives great praise for a scientific paper.

KNOX JOINS the British army. In 1815, he cares for soldiers at the epic Battle of Waterloo.

ROBERT KNOX: Born in 1791. He gets smallpox and loses his sight in one eye, but this doesn't slow him down.

AT EDINBURGH'S university, he works hard to become a doctor but also finds time to have fun.

KNOX GOES to Paris, France, and studies with Georges Cuvier, the world's best anatomist (a scientist who studies bodies).

Silhouette of
Dr. Knox

Handy Hint

Keep counting! As a student in Edinburgh, you'll have to cut up three bodies before you can qualify to be a doctor.

LOOKING GOOD. Friends describe Knox as a strong, well-built person. He loves to wear expensive, fashionable clothes—even while giving lectures and cutting up dead bodies!

ANATOMY AND Physiology.

Notice advertising
Dr. Knox's lectures, 1828

IN 1826, KNOX becomes head of the anatomy school in Edinburgh.

DEAD WRONG. Dr. Knox had ideas about race that turned out to be completely wrong—and are now considered offensive.

RETURNING to Edinburgh, Knox becomes a Fellow of the Royal Society of Edinburgh—a top scientific honor.

KNOX TAKES charge of—and adds to—the famous collection of preserved body parts at Surgeon's Square, Edinburgh.

9

More Modern Medicine

Traditionally, medicine has been divided between doctors (or "physicians") and barber-surgeons. Barber-surgeons stitched cuts and amputated limbs. They were craftsmen, rather than educated professionals. Physicians mostly treated people with medicines. But times have changed, and now—thanks to the medical schools in Edinburgh and other European cities—there's a growing group of trained medical doctors who can perform surgery.

Eyeballs in a jar? Oh, how deliciously ghastly!

Educated surgeons include Scottish brothers William and John Hunter, who became famous in London. When John died in 1793, he left an amazing collection of 10,563 specimens of body parts! London even has public exhibitions of specimens preserved in glass jars. They are educational—and this shocking form of entertainment brings in lots of money.

Handy Hint

Keep your specimens safe! William Hunter built a house that had both a private museum and a room for dissecting bodies!

What am I removing, again?

PROGRESS. In the past 50 years, the scientific study of bodies has helped to improve many medical treatments, such as pulling rotten teeth.

This might hurt...

A CUT ABOVE. Surgeons have learned how to cut bullets out of muscles and stitch up gunshot wounds.

SCIENTISTS like Edward Jenner (1749–1823) have experimented with new techniques for fighting killer diseases, such as vaccinating people against smallpox.

SURGEON William Hunter (1718–1783) became an expert on childbirth. He was made physician to Queen Charlotte and professor of anatomy at the Royal Academy of Arts.

ANIMAL ART. Rich families like portraits of their favorite horses. Some animal artists dissect the huge animals to help learn how to draw them accurately.

BEASTLY. Farmers today are breeding new, bigger animals, and they want portraits of them. But you'll have to paint these prize beasts alive!

NEED FOR SPEED. If you're using dead bodies as models, you have to paint very quickly. They rot—and smell dreadful—after just a few days.

DISPOSAL. Once you've finished with the dead body, you have to get rid of it— without attracting attention.

All for Art

T here is another group of people who investigate bodies— painters and sculptors. Along with my fellow journalists, I've visited their studios and learned a lot. Today's artists like to create realistic portraits, heroic events from myths, or action-packed battle scenes. Many artists pay living models to pose for them.

Can you raise the body's arm up a little?

But some painters feel they need to go a step further in understanding the human body before they can create convincing images. So they have dead bodies secretly delivered to their studios. They cut up the bodies to study the bones and muscles under the skin, hoping to make their paintings more lifelike.

Handy Hint

Travel abroad! See the famous waxworks museum in Florence. It has 19 life-size model human bodies to study. They say that the artists had to study 200 real corpses to make each one of them!

13

Don't Do That!

What's that you say? You want to get a body to examine? Oh no! Take my advice—don't do that!

Why? Because most bodies supplied to doctors, scientists, and artists have been stolen from graves! According to the law, only the bodies of dead criminals can be dissected—and there are not enough of them to go around. Fewer than 100 men and women were hanged in Britain last year, but doctors need ten times that number.

There are criminals—professional body snatchers or "resurrectionists"—who dig up corpses from cemeteries. But they're vicious and violent! Do you really want to meet them?

Moving a Snatched Body

Cram it into sacks or baskets.

Bundle it inside boxes or barrels.

Stuff it under straw in a cart.

Tie it up and label it, like a package.

Other Ways to Snatch a Body

STEAL IT in broad daylight from an isolated churchyard.

TAKE THE RECENTLY deceased from the house of a grieving family.

Wheesht! Weech thon boggin body out!
(Be quiet! Take that revolting body quickly!)
Handy Hint
Think long distance! Bodies used for study have been shipped from Ireland to Scotland, preserved in brine (salt water) or brandy.

Rest in Peace?

No one wants their dead loved ones dug up for dissection. Many people fear that the dead whose graves are unlawfully disturbed will never rest in peace. They also worry about what might happen to their own bodies after they die. For them, the thought of having their bodies snatched is almost worse than death itself. A body robbed from a grave has no name, no past, and no future.

Body-snatching is distressing, offensive, and against the law. So families and communities do all they can to stop this loathsome crime!

SHELL OUT. Pay for a thick lead casket that's too heavy for body snatchers to carry away.

Wee Aunt Mabel was heavier than she looked!

Security Systems

LOCK UP. Put iron straps and locks around wooden coffins. That will keep the lid closed securely.

FENCE IN. Surround churchyards and cemeteries with high walls and spiked metal gates.

KEEP WATCH. Build towers in burial grounds, so that lookouts can watch for thieves.

LOCK IN. Put strong iron bars or cages around individual graves or family plots.

BLOCK OUT. Huge stone slabs make it hard for body snatchers to dig into a grave.

HIRE HELP. Pay tough security guards to patrol and protect graveyards every night.

DIG DEEP. Ask for your loved ones to be buried extra-deep. If snatchers dig too far down, the sides of the graves will cave in and bury them.

Handy Hint

Guard a new grave! Flowers or wreaths will show snatchers where a fresh body has been buried—and will hide traces of grave robbers.

STAY CLEAR of body snatchers! Some people say that you are unlikely to catch nasty diseases from people who handle dead bodies, but do you really want to take the chance?

Filthy Rich

Being a body snatcher is difficult and dangerous—so why do people do it? Because body snatchers make an awful lot of money! In just one night of grimy grave-robbing, a body snatcher can earn almost as much as an honest farm worker makes in a year.

Doctors charge high fees to patients and students, so they can afford to pay for bodies. Most medical men don't want to break the law, but a few get carried away by their passion for science, their rivalry with other researchers, or their love of fame. They become so obsessed with dissecting that they don't stop to ask—and don't want to know— where the dead bodies come from.

DIRTY DEALS. Dealing with body snatchers will make you a criminal. Your medical career will be over before it has even started—and your life will be in danger from mob attacks.

PUBLIC OUTCRY. Doctors and students in Glasgow, Scotland, have been attacked by the outraged families of victims of body snatchers. Now these medical professionals have to be guarded by soldiers!

Money Troubles

Body-snatching is profitable, but snatchers don't get to keep all the money:

TWO'S COMPANY. Body snatchers have to share the cash with their partners—or else they might also end up as dead bodies!

PAY-OFF. They have to pay bribes to curious people who ask awkward questions.

RISKY. They are in constant danger of blackmail from anyone who suspects them or might betray them.

HIGH DEMAND. Prices for bodies are rising. It's the law of supply and demand. As medicine, science, and art become more popular and respectable, there are not enough legally supplied dead bodies to go around.

19

A Steady Supply

William and Margaret Hare

Body snatchers are finding that they can't keep up with demand. After all, you can't really predict how many people will die in any given week. And corpses of the elderly are often unsuitable for dissection. Because of these difficulties, body snatchers are looking for new places to find corpses. Right now, in 1828, it's rumored that they are trying to ensure a steady supply of bodies by killing people!

I suppose murder is quicker and less risky than digging up graveyards. On the other hand, I've heard that two suspected murderers have just been arrested. Their names are—let me look at my notebook—William Burke and William Hare. Both have sold bodies to Dr. Knox!

William and Helen Burke

SHADY PASTS. Rumor has it that Burke's first wife and their children mysteriously disappeared. Hare is suspected of murdering his landlord. Now the two men share a house in Edinburgh with their wives, and take in lodgers.

IRELAND TO EDINBURGH. William Burke (born 1792) and William Hare (born 1790) are both Irish laborers. Like many other poor people, they have come to Scotland to find work. They've done all kinds of odd jobs but don't seem to have earned much money.

EDINBURGH

DOCTOR
Handy Hint
Try to stay alive! Body snatchers get the best price (around £10–15 or $30–50) for healthy young men, just like you!
Whar deed ye get this ane? Its bowfin!
(Where did you get this one? It's very smelly!)
Dinnae worry aboot it. Let's jist say it wis a steal.
(Don't worry about that. Let's just say it was very easy.)

No Evidence?

’ve heard that Burke and Hare found a way of killing that left no marks on their victims. So even if a dissected body was traced back to them, no one could prove that it was murder.

So how did they get caught? It seems that two lodgers in Burke and Hare's house, James and Ann Gray, alerted the police to the duo's shady actions. Another lodger heard strange shouts one night; the next day, Burke was acting suspiciously. So the Grays searched the house and found a body hidden in the bed! Now both men have been arrested.

SECRET SIGNAL. In their crowded lodging house, Helen Burke and Margaret Hare could not say out loud that they had found a new victim to kill. So they gave a secret signal: they stood close to Burke and Hare and under the cover of their long skirts, gently stepped on their husbands' toes.

Typical Tactics

HELEN BURKE and Margaret Hare help the murderers by finding and befriending victims.

THEY FIND a likely victim in the Edinburgh streets and invite them into their house to sit and rest by the fire.

THEY FETCH Burke or Hare and introduce the victim.

THEY GIVE their victim a strong alcoholic drink to relax and confuse them.

SOON, the victim becomes dizzy, sleepy, and completely helpless.

Handy Hint

Stay on your guard! Even though Burke and Hare are in prison, there are plenty more body snatchers still at work.

BURKE and Hare invite the victim to lie down and rest a while.

WHILE THE VICTIM is fast asleep, they creep up and kill them!

Zzzzzz

How Many?

ood to see you again! You're not looking so well! I can see that the body-snatcher murders have shocked you—as they have the rest of us!

Both Burke and Hare claim to be innocent and accuse each other of the crimes. A date has been set for their trial—everyone in Edinburgh thinks they are guilty.

Some of the Victims

A stranger from Glasgow

A woman arrested for being drunk. Burke volunteered to look after her.

Mary Paterson, a pretty young runaway

An English traveler, far from home

Joseph the Miller; he's old, sick, and feeble

A very old woman who came to drink with Burke and Hare

Her 12-year-old grandson, who was deaf

An Edinburgh beggar woman, cold and half-starving

No one knows how many people Burke and Hare have killed. Some say 16, some say 17, some say 30! It seems that all their victims were strangers, outcasts, homeless, weak, or helpless. Most had no family or friends to protect them. Isn't that tragic?

Have you heard? Hare has confessed to the killings, in return for a royal pardon. Only Burke will stand trial—but Hare will still have to face the angry public!

Handy Hint!

Give to charity! The Burke and Hare murders have revealed how many poor people live in Edinburgh's Old Town.

Mrs. Ostler, a poor, hardworking washerwoman

A female friend of Burke's family who was alone in the city

Mary Haldane, a poor old homeless woman

Another female family friend from faraway Ireland

Mary Haldane's daughter Peggy, who was looking for her mother at Burke's house

Mary Docherty, a poor young woman...

Innocent Victims

LONDON, 1831: Body snatchers Bishop and Williams also choose the poor and homeless as their victims. But when they take a well-known homeless child, nicknamed "the Italian Boy," people notice. He is reported missing, and Bishop and Williams are arrested.

Justice Is Done

In December 1828, Burke is tried for multiple murders and found guilty. He is hanged in January 1829 on High Street in Edinburgh. A crowd of 25,000 gather to watch, all shouting insults.

Before Burke's trial, most doctors, scientists, and artists probably hadn't stopped to think where the bodies they used had come from. Now they have been forced to face an unpleasant truth: our recent medical and scientific progress has relied on a miserable trade.

Hing the murtherar! (Hang the murderer!)

Boo!

I heard Hare got off scot free!

I used to be in the medical profession, you know.

HELEN BURKE has been freed but remains under suspicion. The court said her crime was "not proven." She's escaped from her lodgings, dodged angry crowds, and is on a ship to Australia!

WILLIAM HARE is released from prison in 1829. He has also been attacked and was badly injured. He was last seen begging in Carlisle, England. They say he's heading for London.

MARGARET HARE is going back to Ireland, chased by angry citizens. She's off to Glasgow to catch the first steamship she can. In Ireland, she'll be homeless and a beggar.

EDINBURGH CHILDREN have a new song:

Up the close and down the stair...

...In the house with Burke and Hare...

...Burke's the butcher, Hare's the thief...

...Knox the man who buys the beef!

Handy Hint

Don't hang around body snatchers! Even in Australia, Helen Burke's links with body snatchers make her hated and feared, and her house is burned down by an angry mob.

DR. KNOX. There have been riots outside his Edinburgh house, and students stay away from his classes. Eventually he moves to London to work at the new cancer hospital there.

FITTING END? After the hanging, Burke's body is dissected and put on public display in Edinburgh. Sixty people per minute walk past to see it. Then the skeleton is put on display in the Edinburgh University Medical School. (It's still there today.)

27

After Burke and Hare

London, 1832

Amazingly, something positive has come from the terrible story of Burke and Hare's murders. Three years after Burke was hanged, the British government has decided to pass a new law: the Anatomy Act. It will permit the dissection only of dead bodies that are not claimed by relatives within a reasonable time.

A 21st-century medical classroom

In the British Parliament, London:

Vote for science! Vote for knowledge!

The new law means that there will be a steady, legal supply of bodies from workhouses (homes for the poor) and charity hospitals. The price of stolen bodies is already falling, and body snatchers are going out of business. Now doctors, scientists, and artists can study, learn, and help humanity—without committing any crimes!

Astounding! They can see inside a body while it's still alive!

Handy Hint

Keep looking! The human body is fascinating, with many secrets still to discover. Whatever techniques you choose, follow the spirit of the early doctors!

How Dissection Has Helped

SUPER SCIENCE. Since 1832, legal dissections have helped bring about many medical benefits and advances. Here are just some of them:

- Improved mending of broken bones
- Better, safer operations
- Life-saving emergency treatments
- Skin grafts
- Transplant surgeries
- Safer childbirth

MEDICAL STUDENTS still dissect bodies to learn anatomy and to train for surgery. But new technologies allow doctors and scientists to study bodies in amazing detail *without* cutting them up!

MRI scanner

Electron microscope

Ultrasound

29

Glossary

Anatomy The branch of science that deals with the structure of the body, including bone and muscle structure and how the organs work.

Anatomy Act A law passed by the British Parliament in 1832 that allowed any unclaimed dead bodies to be used for medical dissection.

Barber-surgeon A general doctor who treated the sick with basic operations and herbal medicines. The name comes from medieval times, when a doctor also performed the role of barber.

Deceased A dead person (noun) or describing a dead person (adjective).

Dissection The cutting up of a body to study what is inside.

Electron microscope A type of microscope that uses electrons (parts of atoms) to form an enlarged image.

Lecture An educational speech used to teach large groups of students.

Lodger A person who pays money to live in part of someone else's house.

MRI (Magnetic Resonance Imaging) scanner A piece of medical equipment that is used to see inside the body without cutting it open.

Not proven A verdict in Scottish law that means that there is not enough evidence to find the accused person guilty or not guilty.

Parliament In Great Britain, the place where laws are made.

Physician A medical doctor.

Resurrectionist A nickname for a body snatcher.

Royal pardon The forgiving of a crime by a monarch or state authority, sometimes in return for giving important information about another criminal. A criminal who receives a royal pardon is not punished.

Silhouette A picture that shows only a solid black shape, like a shadow. Silhouettes were a popular form of art in the 19th century.

Smallpox An infectious disease that can cause death. It was one of the first diseases to be prevented using vaccination.

Specimen An example of a living thing, or part of a living thing, used for scientific study.

Transplant surgery A lifesaving operation that replaces an unhealthy organ or body part with a healthy one from another person.

Ultrasound Technology that uses high-frequency sound waves to produce images. It can be used to see an unborn baby inside its mother.

Vaccination The use of a vaccine to prevent disease. A vaccine is a weakened form of a disease, given to a patient to help the body prepare itself to fight off a more serious form of the same disease.

Workhouse A place where poor people were given food and housing in return for doing work.

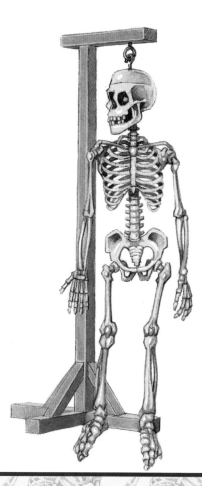

31

Index